ANCIENT AIRS AND DANCES
Suite I

spighi
1936)
David Marlatt

BALLETTO detto "Il conte Orlando"

Allegretto moderato ♩ = 126

ANCIENT AIRS AND DANCES Suite I - BALLETTO pg. 2

ANCIENT AIRS AND DANCES   Suite I - BALLETTO   pg. 3

ANCIENT AIRS AND DANCES
Suite I

Bb Clarinet 1

BALLETTO detto "Il conte Orlando"

Allegretto moderato ♩= 126

O. Respighi
(1879-1936)
Arranged by David Marlatt

ANCIENT AIRS AND DANCES Suite I - BALLETTO pg. 2

ANCIENT AIRS AND DANCES
Suite I

B♭ Clarinet 2

O. Respighi
(1879-1936)
Arranged by David Marlatt

BALLETTO detto "Il conte Orlando"

Allegretto moderato ♩= 126

ANCIENT AIRS AND DANCES   Suite I - BALLETTO   pg. 2

ANCIENT AIRS AND DANCES
Suite I

Bb Clarinet 3

O. Respighi
(1879-1936)
Arranged by David Marlatt

BALLETTO detto "Il conte Orlando"

Allegretto moderato ♩= 126

ANCIENT AIRS AND DANCES Suite I - BALLETTO pg. 2

ANCIENT AIRS AND DANCES
Suite I

Bb Clarinet 4

O. Respighi
(1879-1936)
Arranged by David Marlatt

BALLETTO detto "Il conte Orlando"
Allegretto moderato ♩= 126

ANCIENT AIRS AND DANCES   Suite I - BALLETTO   pg. 2

ANCIENT AIRS AND DANCES
Suite I

B♭ Bass Clarinet

O. Respighi
(1879-1936)
Arranged by David Marlatt

BALLETTO detto "Il conte Orlando"

Allegretto moderato ♩= 126

ANCIENT AIRS AND DANCES   Suite I - BALLETTO   pg. 2